# POEMS

—— *for* ——

# THE BEE CHARMER

• *AND OTHER FAMILIAR GHOSTS* •

# POEMS

—————— *for* ——————

# THE BEE CHARMER

• *AND OTHER FAMILIAR GHOSTS* •

JORDAN LENTZ

*atmosphere press*

# Table of Contents

## • WHAT THE OUTSIDE BROUGHT IN •

# GROWING

———— *into* ————

# HEIRLOOMS

# • 1948 •

What ended in those March flames
awoke from lethargy, years later
marred by inconsistencies and already
worn down in some places,
but audacious and able as ever.

Carrying her old shadow as a purse,
crowned in an aigrette of electric wires
and the choicest shade of rouge
upon her cheeks,
she leaped from the unmistakable feeling
of love, into a new battle—

harder this time,
old foes and cruxes
not yet forgotten

but not yet important either.

## • VAN GOGH •

Pollen pools in the corner of my eyes
like stardust seeping in from another life.
I've always wanted to be yellow.

But a color like that eternally asks for more.
It eats your bones into crookedness,
carving a country for itself.
A kind of scalding scoliosis.

My black and blue
from the inside out
is hard to unravel.

Skin ages,
tries to mend, fade to yellow
but I can never offer enough
healing to become.

Now—I am tapping into
your ribs.
Sweat between our skin
like golden ichor
I wish I bled.

Your honeycombs pour
right into my bruises.

# • COMPOSITION •

On that June morning, we are waltzing.
The sunrise and ocean mist tangle in my hair,
I tell him, our hearts beat in ¾ time,
that's why this should feel as
natural as breathing.

On the French Riviera, we are waltzing.
The sand and pebbles between our toes,
he tells me, we are seventy percent water,
that's why when the waves roll in and drift out,
we feel it in our veins.

Mimosas stretching along the coastline,
that ¾ beat knocking on our ribs,
we have little chance of stopping,
our minds being overpowered
by the composition of our bodies.

The ocean tugging us near,
our arms pulsing to the beat of the waltz,
fingertips hot and tingling staccato marks,
we touch the sea, it wraps our ankles,
the water inside us crescendos towards the waves.

I move right instead of left,
I step against the current instead of into it,
the badlands in my bones grow dryer,
my heartbeat quickens, slips into
a rebel ¼ time.

Suddenly I breathe too deep, find myself back in rhythm,
my mind betrayed by the composition again.
My ribs click into place; one more line cracks across my lips,
his hands are steady like a barge; his eyes are focused like a hawk's.
We are waltzing, after all.

# • SONG TO THE SUFFRAGETTES •

Roaring twenties, raging through legislation
rampant, with blood on our hands
to be treated as human men.

Human men, say then,
women have never created anything
their names on no devices, developments, discoveries.

Preferring to see us
pushing daisies instead of planting them
if we have opinions, options, opportunities.

Flinch, flee, flat-line
which is more beautiful
insides out or outsides in?

We prefer the former,
not to be made of galaxies
but to join them.

We want our inside screams out,
our deepest desires, our wildest dreams
streaking across the sky for all to see.

We have felt canyons in our mouths,
badlands in our bones,
seen mirages of equality, let ourselves believe we've made it.

Suffer, suffocate, suffragette
we've never created anything,
but sparks—

Sparks start wildfires.

# • STELLA •

I am your ambrosia.
Pretend again to be a god.

Call my name in the dark.
Let it fill the humid air,
let it twist on coattails of wind,
let it draw circles in the dirt.
Do not dare to call it back, do not dust it off.

When you ask for my forgiveness,
put your thumbs on my hips
and leave imprints of what you call love.
Put your knees atop each pebble on the ground—
let them show you how to feel.
When it hurts enough for both of us, I will let you stand.

Promise you will never promise me anything again.
You do not have to say it, I know:
You will always love me like you never did.

# • THE BEE CHARMER •

Tells me like it is.
She corners my indecisions
and douses them in gasoline
to light a fire of certainty.

The American beech trees
collect love for her.
She builds corridors
from combs and cardamom

as I watch from the front steps.

The bee charmer
sleeps on the backs
of caramelized oak leaves
and calls to me for promises.

But when the rains come,
and spools of pollen
unravel across my knees—
it's time for me to leave.

And she says,
"Call if you need me."

# • THE POWER TO LAUGH ROSES AS I
## WEEP GOLD •

In your garden,
poised on the edge of the small koi pond you tame
with your subtle stitched fingers,
as a spider slickly sews her home with spinnerets.
I watch my reflection ripple across the spines of unsuspecting fish;
my eyes drifting over their whiskers, my lips upon their tails,
like we are suturing pieces of our skin and scales together.

In your garden,
you sit silently on the swing behind me, swaying in the wind,
no radiation in your bloodstream,
no sickness strapping you to a bed.
You watch me drift my fingers over the water
you laugh roses. Sweet, succulent roses.
Their petals fall across your wrinkled arms;
they writhe gently in the breeze,
clean sheets on a laundry line.
I watch the fish, with their kaleidoscope colors
as I weep gold, like Midas
over his sins. Because I have found
the very last corner of earth
I want to be in
when my breath begins
to draw thin.

# • MA BELLE PETITE •

Remember that it's writing until you are bare,
until the papers are strewn across the floor
until you are naked, and it's witching hour.

Try to take it all in—
This is forgiveness.

Speak.
The moon, the demons, are listening.

C'est la vie, ma belle petite.
When this is over, you'll remember more

than pain.

# • CATHERINE •

Cinder-woman in the night
what I believe is true,
what could have been your life
clutched six feet under too

And the lichens took you over
the ground reclaimed your flesh
an unsuspecting ambler
wouldn't give a second glance

And all that once was breathing
their breathing days have been
the steps of loved ones grieving
will cease to come again

If I ever were so lucky
to find the spot you sweetly lay
I'd set my fore upon your headstone
and remind you of your name.

# • HEART •

My body is carved from the bottom of a blue canoe.
The curve of the wood etched out my spine, the knots
whittled themselves into my small crooked vertebrae.
Beneath the wicker seat, sunspots strain upon my face
like a token of gratitude, planting speckled
wildflower seeds above my missing front teeth.

The pale ringlets on my head, sprouted
from the dandelion seeds spread by the wind,
were always swept across your lifejacket.
Your lifejacket, as my pillow—
isn't that the way it has always been

your life, for my comfort?

Water droplets collect on my not-yet-grown legs
as you lift the canoe paddles over your head
over my sunbathing body, back and forth above
the canoe, pulling us across the croaking lily-pad pond,
forward—into the itchy milkweed buds, the fish beds,
the hoards of pirouetting water spiders and moss.
What does it feel like to remember what you are about to lose?

It feels like:

Paddling across a pond to catch bass and pickerel
that you will let go free—paddling until the cicada sun
relaxes into the dusk behind a mountain ridge.
Until you wear your shoulders down to thimbles
and prick your raw and muddy hands into fish hooks
enough for the callouses to grow.

To carry your sleeping daughter, while you still can:
across the retrograde boat launch, with pebbles
pressing into the sore soles of your feet
to carry her to the front seat of the Wrangler,
buckle her into the booster stained with chocolate milk,
and kiss her dandelion head.

# • THE BEE CHARMER, REPRISE •

A dime down the throat
of a payphone.

Still she answers,
after all this time.

# VARIOUS COASTLINES

—————— *and* ——————

# COORDINATES

# • LAUNDRY ROOM •

Sitting here, in my Sunday best,
between all the cotton clouds puffed out by the dryer—
I have never found enough of myself.

At these times I can't stop thinking about
the sound of jet turbines on the west coast,
rattling the California Mountains,
shaking the albatrosses from their trees.
Where I sat with peanuts and Coke between my fingertips, salt
    dusting each
cuticle my hands hold; dancing slightly in my own way,
humming quietly in my economy seat. The LA sunset saturating
    my cheeks
with rouge through the small open
spaces of the plane—

In this laundry room, waiting for something in my life to be clean,
I think about the way the jet turbines sound when they die down,
    when you
get to where you are going. I think about the way they sounded
    sighing to
sleep on the west coast.

I know someday when the time is right I will hear that sound again,
and after my erratic heart slows to a steadfast beat, after
I have seen all that I can see:
I will click my heels; I will come back to these clean sheets.

## • IN THE UNDERGROUND STREETS OF
## NEW YORK •

I sit on a bench; a boy with headphones sits next to me and
watches me bite my lip while I watch in my head the subway
door slam between us. Me on the platform, you on the train. The
boy with headphones is tapping his legs along to his music; I am
tapping my legs along to my nerves, along to the creak of the
tracks as your train pulls away, the scream of the tunnel as it
swallows you whole.

# • PALATINE HILL •

*"I am healing by mistake.*
*Rome is also built on ruins."*
  Eliza Griswold

My skin still sounds like a flame,
like the crackling the spark
in your eyes sang, when I once
told you I was ready to be loved.

I have done nothing but set myself
on fire since you handed me a match.
Nero burned down his own empire,
can't I be nostalgic?

In a wandering way that does not hurt,
I walk around Rome alone at night.
I tread between longing and memory,
and I try not to get them confused.

I am rebuilding myself on top of
this destroyed frame to be stronger
than before, to be everything that
I could not when I was a relic of a girl.

# • ON A BEACH IN LAZIO •

I watch the sun
burn your skin
but you're not really here
and I'm surprised
when that bothers me.

I play tag
with the riptide
but I'm sidetracked
by the color of the waves
or better yet
my friend's flask
taking residence
in my right hand—
Something to pass the time
and make my lips
taste like peach again.

We catch the train back
but not before
walking a mile
and sneaking on
to the local bus
where a man
brushes against me
and laughs when
I push away.

On the way home
I see your face
in every window
feel your hands
in every turnstile—

I look for something better,
to justify being here alone.

Watching the sun
burn the ghost of you,
chasing the riptide
with the thought of you,
walking down
the backstreets of Lazio
with the vision of you
standing beside me.

Standing beside me
on the bus,
telling the old hound
to go fuck himself,
finally landing
a punch for me,
another broken hand
for the road.

But I'm here alone.
And every leaning
of the train
justifies the means
and unravels them
again,
on the next turn.

# • KANANASKIS, ALBERTA •

Melancholy haunts
    The chasms
Remembering falls
    To the mountain goats
There is only snow
    On peaks
But it is Summer
    Down below.

When I am gone
    When I have left this place
My left hand's shadow stays
    Sprigs of dandelion floss, peonies
Between thumb and forefinger
    A potion for years of yearning.

# • SOHIER PARK •

Where the gulls scavenged snails
and the glow from the lighthouse
made you seem far away,
somewhere I couldn't follow.

We took pictures in the dark,
Venus above my head,
the moon above yours.

On New Year's Eve,
we drove across town
to a high school party
and wasted our time
on a game of Kings.

But it wasn't
wasted time to me,
now that I think about it.

Now that I think about it
when you are far away,
somewhere I can't follow.

# • FEBRUARY IN BOSTON •

I was so in love with you then.
Thought I might fold myself
up, small as a paper note,
and let you swallow me,
words and all, veins
and all, bones palpable
and forgiving.

Waiting outside the club
on the curb, blue coat
freckled with white snow,
thought you might have left
me. Men howling in cavalier
cars rush by, then silence
when you walked out the door.

I drove home, legs frozen
to the leather seat, passenger
side occupied with you holding
your love for me on your lap.
Friends in the backseat
felt like strangers
behind the glass of a taxi.

In the night, I woke
to dying embers
in the hearth, empty
sheets, my skin shivered
and see-through. Thought
you might have left me.

Found you in the kitchen
staring through the glass door
at flakes falling in floodlight.
Pulled me to your right hip,
let me watch with you. Gathered
me up in all my goosebumps, arctic
toes off the stone, lips to neck.

Didn't know I needed winter
to feel loved.

# • AMALFI COAST, ALTERNATE TIMELINE •

Spools of thread, melted wax
For one moment we are courageous
Packing the ghosts and the winds
And seeing what makes it

Conversations and muted confessions
Take the dried salt home in your pocket
Take the long way
Admit to vows and cypress rings

Balconies, missing floorboards
The blue kitchen I'd hoped for
Enough cobwebs to weave a duvet
Enough things said to forget

Enough unsaid to remember
But there isn't enough ocean
To separate what did
And didn't happen

# • FOSSIL •

Sandalwood and palm leaves
writhing in the heat.

Trying to grow out of themselves,
into something more.

Part of me is tangled up
in the San Diego coastline.
Lost in those 70 miles
of sand dunes and parted dust.

70 miles of trying to forgive
myself for growing up. 17 years
of trying to find my way
back there,

To claw into
those silt seams
and tear them apart—
Feed them to the sea.

And bury all
of myself
where I left the others,

Forever ago.

# • TRADE WINDS •

Everything I write comes back
to various coastlines,
Familiar ghosts in the bylines
Waiting on the sandbars
for my eyes to track

Reasons for the beach
to look unsightly in the moonlight.
I search for faces in the wave whites,
Ask for forgiveness
that's too far out of reach

And that's enough for now—
That's got to be enough for me.

# SELF-PORTRAIT

—— *hues* ——

# • SOMEDAY •

they all say, "you'll be better someday.
someday you won't want to rip your skin in half and climb out.
you won't feel the searing desire to release all the oxygen from your
     lungs
and float up to the iridescent balloon in the sky (where the free
     people live
and ideas run wild)
where you can dangle your bare innocent feet off the side and
get sprinkled with the blush of giggling stars
as they wander by
on their way to find a new universe."

it's hard to wait for someday.
and it's nearly impossible to reach tomorrow
when your lungs are leaking and your feet are slowly lifting (from
     where they should want to be)
off the ground
and your head is spinning.

but you inhale and tell yourself
*someday*
the iridescent balloon in the sky
(the one where you would find peace at last—amongst the
floating orbs of fire and endless streams of consciousness
and abysmal craters with cracked paths (the ones that hold the
     secrets);
the place where all the pieces of yourself you have lost
the stars would carry back to you and you would be whole again)
will become much less enticing.

and another day, that searing desire will return
(but only when your somedays have passed)
and the stars will beckon you home
(and you will answer at last).

# • WHEN I DID NOT WISH FOR AN ANTIDOTE •

still i cannot forget the badlands. how they echoed every word i
spoke within their walls, how i am still trapped in between those
honey rusted hills. my leg bitten by a snake and the poison
steeping slowly in my bloodstream like a tea bag in boiling water.
i heard the desert say *you are here now, you are home* and i knew
not to run. *my dust with yours forever,* i responded, and laid
down in pillows of sand. it is possible i was never there at all.

# • HUMAN AGAIN •

That feeling, I know well.
It is not anything more than dancing by myself;
in the middle of summer
with the window breathing
above the sink,
in the parched kitchen,
next to a canyon of dirty dishes,
linoleum floor rising and
falling beneath the pads of my feet
because of the heat,
because of the way it was put in wrong.

Orange-scented dish soap bubbles
floating past my parted lips,
the radio singing about heartbreak,
me: dancing with bubbles on my arms,
remembering to drain the sink,
when the water gets brown,
remembering to turn the music down,
when my mother pulls in the driveway.

# • I AM SPENDING TIME WITH MY BODY •

I am spending time with my body
because she will be taken away
from me soon, skin I have been learning
to love for years soon to be removed.
I used to carve this skin, I engraved
the fat on my thighs with railroad tracks.
It's taken me years to want this skin,
I have earned this skin and I will not
be handing her over to a man
with grubby hands just to be hated
all over again.

I am spending time with my body
because she will not be mine for long.
I am pinching the rolls and folds on my
stomach between my fingers and apologizing for ever
trying to get rid of them, years of
leaning over a toilet seat taught
me the way to feel hungry and I
will not be letting you anywhere
near this body now that it is loved
and finally full.

I am getting to know every chink
and crevice before they are filled in
by crooks, I have three freckles on my
left cheek. I think I will miss them greatly.
I talked to my uterus around
breakfast this morning and she told me
democracy is dead. She died late
last night in my womb and
emerged at daybreak in a cluster
of fascism, battered and bloody

with century-old wounds the suffragettes
thought they healed.

## • WHEN I STILL HAVE NOT FOUND THE PIPE
## MY SHADOW GOT CAUGHT IN •

*All that I know is I'm breathing now.* Singing between porcelain
walls and the blue and yellow tiles as the wind screams against the
faux stained glass window. *All we can do is keep breathing.* She
sings. I read *A Prayer for Owen Meany* in the bathtub for three
and a half hours over Christmas break. I am young enough and
my thighs are still sticks. Owen Meany is talking about a red dress
on a figurine and putting cars in gyms but I am in the bathroom in
the old haunted apartment on Main Street with 63 rubber ducks
accompanying me on various shelves, in the closet, on the back of
the toilet, the sink. It is winter in here and my skin is the surface
of the moon if the moon had rain. I pull the plug and wait until
only my pruned toes are submerged to stand and grab my towel.
At last, the bathtub takes its final gulp, swallows my shadow, and I
start my Peter Pan chase to find a way to keep breathing under all
this age.

# • PLEISTOCENE •

Secrets and gnats
intertwining off the glacial coast.
Tongues over limbs,
carbon arms fading to the wayside.

Tetrachloride powerless
without a flame to bite.
But then, what must I make of this,
if I must make something?

I can think in nothing
but confessions, these days.
Humming in minors as I dance
across this truth-riddled half-life,

Into the arms of a ghost. Until
I'm yelling my findings into the chasm,
breathless for an echoed response—

And dancing wilder in the silence.

# • FEATHERWEIGHT •

*"They are not brave, the days when we are twenty-one."*
                        Daphne du Maurier

I don't feel
brave tonight.

Moving around
from the waist down,
turning twenty-one
over in my mind.
Turning cherry stems
over in my mouth.

I don't feel brave tonight.
I feel tragic,
almost divine. I feel
the need to get down
on my knees and pray
for the return of winter,
pray for snow.

Turning twenty-one
with only strangers
by my side,
corduroy thighs
walking next to me
through the parking garage
and into the house.

I invite you upstairs
to forget about him.
Remember, I don't
feel brave tonight
and everything is to be
lost for us.

Moving around
from the waist down,
only find sleep for
twenty-one minutes
then wake to find
searching limbs
in the dark, to find
I haven't grown
enough for this.

# • SATURN •

Saturn makes noise when no one's around.
I would like to do that too.
Why be silent when you could
be a million wind chimes
singing for themselves?

# • *STARS AND STRIPES FOREVER* •

When I was young
And a blush was
A conviction,
I pardoned you
From all crimes
But kept a copy
Of the stenographer's
Notes

To read in the
Failing lamplight
Of the library,
Behind the M
through N shelf,
Back against
Dust graffitied
Bricks.

When I was young
And a blush was
A conviction,
You pardoned me
From all crimes
But kept a copy
Of the stenographer's
Notes

To read in the
Floodlight of
The football field,
Beside the fifty
Yard line,
Back against
Dew-ridden
grass.

When we were young
And love was
The hallway
Between classes,
Was the sound
Of dizzy laughter
From the back
Row

Where we
Traced notes
Into each other's
Palms, underlined
Quotes in
Secondhand
Copies of *Owen
Meany.*

When we were young
And love was
The hallway
Between classes,
Was the sound
Of dizzy laughter
From the back
Row

Where we
Passed time
To each other,
Gave up hope
For one another,
When the secrets
Hurt too
much.

And on Saturdays
You watched
My lips hum
*Stars and Stripes*
*Forever* in
The marching
Band stands
Before

I mounted
The tightrope,
Climbed up
The ladder
To my act,
As the rest of
The band played
on.

And on Saturdays
You watched
My lips hum
*Stars and Stripes*
*Forever* in
The marching
Band stands
Before

You tried not
To sing along
While in the
Arms of another,
Tried not to
Climb up the
Ladder to my
Act.

And so it went:
Time turning
Days into years,
Eyes turning
Towards me,
My eyes
For you
Only

As I laid
Upon that
Tightrope,
As I cast out,
Caught myself
In the beat
Back and the
rise.

And so it went:
Time turning
Days into years,
Eyes turning
Towards me,
My eyes
For you
Only

As you laid
Upon her bed,
As you called
From the
Sheets, for me
Gave hope to
The ghost of
me.

Like the trapezist
Frightened but still swinging
When the disaster march
Strikes up

I kept going
Around and around
And around
And around

For you.

Like the trapezist
Frightened but humming along
When the disaster march
Strikes up

I kept going
Around and around
And around
And around

For you.

# • EPILOGUE FOR EMILY •

One ghost have I in my house—
And one in my head.
Though both belong to me,
I don't know which of us is dead.

The creaking upon rotting boards
That haunts into the night
Has a way to draw me towards
The terrors out of sight.

Is it my own bare padding feet
That trek all down the hall?
Or is it the ghost under the sheet
That creeps and wakes us all?

One ghost have I in my house—
And one in my head.
Though both belong to me,
I don't remember how we met.

The one in my bedroom corner
Has yet to say her name
But every night I mourn for her
And call her just the same.

The days are long enough to feel
As though they'll never end
I burn, I break, I scream, I steal
And try my best to mend.

A thing most certainly hard to do
With ghosts in house and head.

# • CONSECRATION •

I carried consecration
like a pearl.
White and smooth,
opal, undecided,
sacred to a mouth
in the sea, parted by
passing waves.

If you have ever
tasted salt,
you know
the afterthought
of being holy.

# WHAT THE

—— *outside* ——

# BROUGHT IN

# • PRESENTLY •

A mist is sleeping upon the lakeshore.
My well-worn lips are tenderly slipping
from yours, resisting desire for more,
turning away, towards the sound of dripping—

The requiem of rain, bleeding off pines,
trickling onto the pebbles of the coast.
A song so lovely it cannot be mine
marble girls meander, silent as ghosts.

This is a lake, but I wanted a sea,
'tis debauchery, instead of a throne.
Crescent clamshells are not enough for me
yet you rest them upon my collarbone.

Your pleasure is ample for the moment,
be warned—I find more thrill in atonement.

# • PEREGRINE •

To the solemn lakeside,
to the winter shed.
Whatever is left unsaid
we will leave to the birds—
But for now, we have
enough time to pretend
to say something true.

When this unravels itself
I'll be sitting
in a parched desert
without so much
as a stray thought.

To regret and to have loved
are the same thing.
And I think, always worth it
in the end.

## • *BOTH SIDES NOW,* EPILOGUE •

A honeybee in its honey hive,
working for the right words to say.
Oh honey, I think I may die,
from the sweetness of it all.

A woman paces in fading yellow light,
in some city beyond the horizon.
As I stand here,
with bated breath and baby's breath,
and juniper berries between my hands.
She untangles her hair from a braid,
and decides it would look better these days,
chopped off like Greta Garbo's in 1925.
I bleed into the vase.
I think I could let it go; I could let them go;
I could make our trash smell sweet.

I never stop thinking about the beach
when I'm in the forest.
The cicadas sound like seagulls to me,
and I pretend to be alone.

I pretend to forget
that nonsensical way we moved.
The way Joni told us to,
that *dizzy dancing way* that we feel,
I haven't felt, I haven't felt.
I never told you
never
this is not the feeling I write poems
about.
But *I've looked at love from both sides now,*
and either way it isn't fair.

If I tried to write about you, the ink
would be the thread of the very spindle of my soul.
And I'm not sorry that I love myself enough,
to look at love alone.

# • RECKONING •

If I'm being haunted
I want it to be by you

A ghost that knows
What my head on
Your shoulder feels like.

I'll try not to flinch
When I hear you close the door

Your presence is just something
So oddly romantic
They haven't a name
For it yet.

# • SEULEMENT TOI •

If you knocked
On my door
Right now

I know
That I would
Let you in

Regardless of
The countless 'NO!s'
Echoing in my head.

For some reason
You are worth
More than

1
2
3

Tries.

In fact,
I think
I'd let you in my door
At least a million times.

(Come back a million and one
So I can finally be done.
Seulement toi,
Seulement toi.)

# • CARRIED AWAY •

Dancing in unusual places
anywhere
I can get my hands on you.

Creature of habit limbs
forget
what to do in the kitchen
and only remember
what to do in the arms
of the beat.

Sweltering in the oasis
of the oven
illuminated in the neon vigil
of the refrigerator.

Let the rest
burn and burn and burn.

I can remake anything
in this kitchen
but you.

# • RED AND REMEMBERING •

I am drunk
and you
are better
at talking to me
than I remember.

I can run
all night
in my heels
if you want to—

I have so very
much I could
run away to.
And you

have never been
my ex lover
my ex significant other
an extraordinary anything

in my life when
the circumstances were
right. Now, all at once, you
have become them wholly.

I am drunk
and God, if you could
please pour another gin
I will gulp it down, I—

want to stumble home
I want to
fall and scrape my
knees on the asphalt, I—

want to bleed
into my sheets
tonight, to wake up
in the morning, alone,

red and remembering.

# • IN MY MIND •

The memory of your voice cracking, at one o'clock in the morning,
right against the supple stitching of my ear where it hurts most,
still sounds like my heart is being put on a carousel.

It sounds like the way I would try a cigarette once,
give it one chance to kill me. Like my grandmother when she was
    sixteen,
when she trod down the eager sidewalk into the drugstore,

bought a pack of Marlboros and smoked it on the bus ride home,
puffing out smolder from her mouth like the rattling exhaust from
    the muffler, extinguished the last one after planting a seed of
    malignancy in her lungs.

My own lungs still hold your breath tightly within themselves
from when I almost let you kiss me. You exhaled on my lips that
    late night,
between those telling walls, but I never tried you, not once.

The way this vicarious impulse is the thing that makes us so human,
the way we have a different configuration with every inhale, new
    manifestations
of mass, new clumps of cells, new blood to clot our unraveling
    wounds

and yet I still can't shake that old part of you stuck inside me.
I only hope we may sometime meet again and I shall be able, perhaps,
to say what I cannot write.

# • *WHEN HARRY MET SALLY* •

Made you cry for the first time.
Paused in the retro hallway,
leaning on the wall. You said,
*I don't want that*
*to happen to us.*

I didn't understand it then,
what you meant. But
I did one year later,
stopping for breath
in January
after seeing you,
for the first time after.

I understand it now,
every time I board a plane,
every time sitting by myself
on the way somewhere new.

Every time I rewatch
that movie, and think,
*How could they ever*
*let that happen to them?*

# • DEAD MEN TELL NO TALES •

When the summer sickness doesn't fade
With the end of September
I know something is wrong.

I'm playing dead, I'm playing
The long game
To spill it all in the end.

As October fades into itself
And fury turns you a color
I'm afraid of

I'm ready to reveal
Any secret I'm meant to keep.

Like how when I think
Something could last forever
I wrap it in pearls
And toss it overboard.

Or how I still
Think of him.

Or how, after all this time,
The smell of eucalyptus salve
Brings me back to that night

Down by the lake, back to
The breaking ice and his hand
Close enough, his winter breath
Near my ear, and the look of love—

No—
Some things
You should take to the grave.

# • SMALL LOVE •

*"As it has been said:*
*Love and a cough*
*Cannot be concealed.*
*Even a small cough.*
*Even a small love."*
  Anne Sexton

The mystery of that hatred,
which built inside me
those winter months of eighteen,
I can't answer for—

But I can tell you
your palms were countries
I longed to explore.

And that hatred, which
I now believe
was just love undisclosed,
still digs under my rib cage.

Still carves a home for itself
where I have no room
to spare, and burns
late into each night.

Do you remember?
Each night, spent cut from
the same cloth. Each way
we reeled when it was all over.

When it was all over.

That placebo I rebuilt
my bones from, out of
the coveted veins
of the boy upstairs—

That sober regret
the next day, which turned
into months, which turned
into nothing more

than time gone by
with you
on the other side of the wall.

In my dreams,
he forgives me
and you do too.

And as it has been said:
even now, I cannot forget,
I cannot conceal the burning
for what could have been mine.

But you're just
a small love.
One that's too big to hide
in the cupboard
beside my other skeletons.

But a small love
that still burns
all the same.

## • MEMORY NEVER DOES ENOUGH FOR ME •

Memory never does enough
for me, yet always more
than the presence of the present.

Writing feels more successful
in the past.
Captured better when

I was young and sat
upon my grandfather's chair
scribbling into the pages of Spring!

Watching the world
melt into itself
outside the open window

—And again, and again, it becomes,
even earlier today in the halo
of sunshine off the winter snow...

I wrote so much better than now!

Love never fits me, unless
it is an echo, of
something spoken long ago,

On the coast, you uttered vows
in your sleep and I wound
them up in spindles of dreams...

I loved so much better than now!

And those times
that I remember,
of when I was better

All fall upon
each other, like clothes
hung from a Venetian line

And my nostalgia pulls
them down, as the wind
tugs the threads into the canals.

Isn't it funny
who is responsible for
the falling of things?

Now, my bedroom is dark
and sweet-smelling
of lemongrass.

I'll write a verse! Or
perhaps we shall go
and have another moment,

One I will not enjoy
until your shirt falls
off the line, onto…

My moonbeam lap,
softer than I remember.
In years to come?

When you
are not here
no more,

and my heart has finally grown fond.

# —— About Atmosphere Press ——

Atmosphere Press is an independent, full-service publisher for excellent books in all genres and for all audiences. Learn more about what we do at atmospherepress.com.

We encourage you to check out some of Atmosphere's latest releases, which are available at Amazon.com and via order from your local bookstore:

*Reflections in the Time of Trumpius Maximus*, poetry by Mark Fishbein

*Drifters*, poetry by Stuart Silverman

*As a Patient Thinks about the Desert*, poetry by Rick Anthony

*Winter Solstice*, poetry by Diana Howard

*Songs of Snow and Silence*, poetry by Jen Emery

*INHABITANT*, poetry by Charles Crittenden

*Godless Grace*, poetry by Michael Terence O'Brien

*March of the Mindless*, poetry by Thomas Walrod

*In the Village That Is Not Burning Down*, poetry by Travis Nathan Brown

*Mud Ajar*, poetry by Hiram Larew

*To Let Myself Go*, poetry by Kimberly Olivera Lainez

*I Am Not Young And I Will Die With This Car In My Garage*, poetry by Blake Rong

# About the Author

Jordan Lentz was raised in the small New Hampshire town of Rollinsford, and grew up fascinated with books, mythology and archaeology. One sleepless night at the age of sixteen, she wrote her first poem in her childhood bedroom. Armed with this new love of writing and old love of the past, Lentz pursued a double major in English and Anthropology at the University of Vermont where she graduated in 2019. Lentz currently works as a middle school English teacher in Providence, Rhode Island where she lives with her two cats.